IMAGES
of England

SHIRLEY
AND
ADDINGTON

Reading Copy

Publication date: JANUARY 03

1st Edition: ☑   Reprint: ☐

Number of copies: 900

Shirley windmill within the grounds of John Ruskin school in 1987.

IMAGES
of England

SHIRLEY
AND
ADDINGTON

Raymond Wheeler

JANUARY

TEMPUS

Frank Still owned dairies in South Norwood High Street and in Cherry Orchard Road, Croydon. Milk was supplied from the dairy herd kept at Shirley Park Farm on the opposite side of the road to Shirley House. This photograph shows a handcart used for milk deliveries in around 1906. The ladles were used to transfer milk into cans for delivery.

First published 2003

Tempus Publishing Limited
The Mill, Brimscombe Port,
Stroud, Gloucestershire, GL5 2QG

British Library Cataloguing in Publication Data.
A catalogue record for this book is available from the British Library.

ISBN 0 7524 2683 4

Typesetting and origination by Tempus Publishing Limited
Printed in Great Britain by Midway Colour Print, Wiltshire

Contents

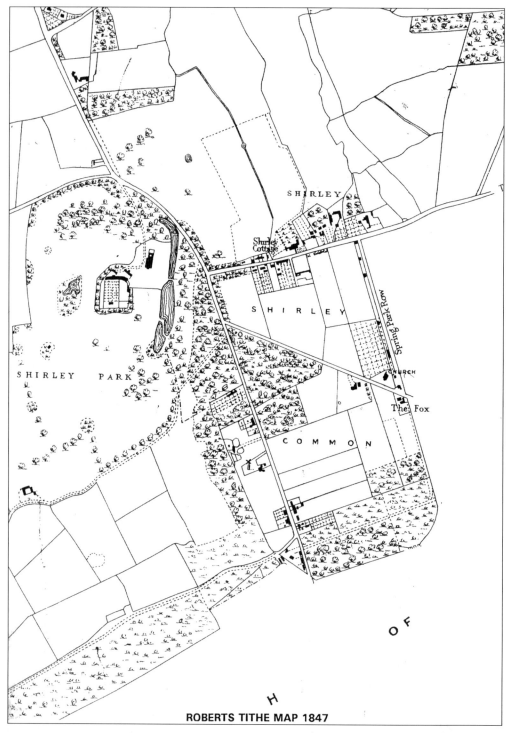

ROBERTS TITHE MAP 1847

An extract from *The Tithe Map of Croydon*, drawn by W. Roberts in 1847.

Introduction

A relative once challenged me 'What possible history is there in Shirley?'. With that comment, and others made to me through the exhibition mounted for the fortieth anniversary of All Saints (Spring Park) church in 1996, the seed of this book was sown.

Shirley lies on the lower slopes of an east-west ridge, extending from Ballards to Shirley Heath, rising to over 140 metres comprising sands and gravel of the Tertiary Age. Coarse gravel of rounded pebbles of the Blackheath Beds outcrop lie on the ridge while on the lower northern slopes the underlying strata comprise the Woolwich and Thanet Beds and, further north, London clay. At the junction of the Blackheath Beds and the Woolwich Beds is a spring line from which issue streams draining north. Those visible today are the River Bec and the springs forming Miller's Pond. Others feed into the Chaffinch Brook.

It was in Saxon times that Shirley was named, though there is not complete agreement about what the name means. Originally either *Scyr-Leaze* or *Sheer-Leaze* from *Leah* meaning 'meadow' or 'pasture', and *Scyr* meaning 'boundary', or *Sheer* meaning 'bright', hence Shirley meant originally 'Bright Meadow' or 'The pasture by the boundary'. In the Domesday Book of 1086 Shirley is mentioned as 'a Manor of Ham, near Croydon' and was owned by the Count of Mortain. In the seventeenth century Shirley was a small hamlet along the ancient route from Croydon to West Wickham, situated on the edge of the common near to where Shirley House was to be built.

Before the Croydon Enclosure Act of 1797 was passed, the area south of the Wickham Road comprised Shirley Common which, in the early nineteenth century, was covered in 'short heath and furze and cannot be said to be worth more than 1s 6d per acre.' After enclosure of the common, the population began to grow and centred around the new settlement of Upper Shirley. In 1810 a windmill was built, then a chapel in 1836 (a church in 1856), and a brewery. Many villagers worked in the sandpits. Shirley became a desirable place for gentlemen of means to have their country estates such as Shirley House, Ham, Spring Park, and Monks Orchard. The Eldon's at Shirley House and Lewis Loyd at Monks Orchard were benefactors of the church and village. Later into the nineteenth century, Shirley became a popular tourist attraction for Londoners, with Addington Hills effectively becoming the 'Hampstead Heath of the south'.

Tremendous changes took place during the post-war era. Ham and Spring Park were sold off for housing as well as land around Shirley House, which became the Shirley Park Hotel. Milling, brewing and working on the estates were no longer means of employment. Shirley became a commuting community. Since the Second World War, further changes have taken place: Shrublands has been built on part of Addington New Golf Course, the Shirley Oaks children's home has been replaced by the new Shirley Oaks housing estate; new schools and in-fill development has taken place in the Ham Farm area, and retirement flats have been built. Thankfully, though, the generosity of past landowners ensured that the rising tide of bricks and mortar would not entirely engulf Shirley. Many acres of green space remain through the preserved woodlands, golf courses and public open spaces.

The village of Addington, three and a half miles from Croydon, lies in a valley formed by the Addington Hills to the north and the slopes of the North Downs to the south. One of the smallest villages in England in 1850, by 1960 Addington still retained its rural character. Evidence of pre-Roman settlement has been found but the village dates from Saxon times. Its name probably derives from the Anglo-Saxon *Aeddi's tun* – Aeddi being a landowner and the tun, his farm, on top of the hill to the north.

Domesday Book records that in the time of Edward the Confessor, Addington was divided into two manors: Osward held Eddintone and Godric held Edintone, whose lands were handed over by William the Conqueror to Albert the Clerk and Tezelin the Cook respectively. It is not possible to delineate accurately the two holdings, but Albert's manor lay to the south, probably based on the combined areas of Addington Lodge Farm and Castle Hill Farm (now New Addington). Tezelin's holding comprised the northern part of the parish including the manorial park, church and village centre.

Various families held the manors of Addington during the succeeding centuries, including de Chesney, Aguillon and Bardolph. By Tudor times Nicholas Leigh had come into possession of the whole of the parish of Addington. The Leighs remained lords of the manor until 1768 when Addington was purchased by Barlow Trecothick. A new phase in the history of Addington began in 1807 when Addington Place was sold to the Archbishops of Canterbury and the house thereafter became known as Addington Palace.

A number of buildings survive from its village days: the church of St Mary the Virgin, the smithy and the Cricketer's Inn are reminders of years past. In 1972 the by-pass opened taking 16,000 cars a day out of the village. Its designation as a Conservation Area has ensured a rural atmosphere.

In contrast, New Addington has grown considerably over the last sixty years since the construction of the first National Housing Trust estate. New schools, churches, shops, factories, a swimming pool and a library have contributed to a strong community spirit. The opening of Tramlink has considerably improved transport links with Croydon and made the district more accessible for the 30,000 plus residents.

To the north, Addington Hills is now a public open space and the estate of Heathfield on the ridge by Addington Hills remains intact, again open for the enjoyment of all. The open aspect of Ballards – also on the ridge – leads down to the area of Coombe, whose ancient mansions, only a couple of miles from the centre of Croydon, retain their historic integrity, albeit they are now restaurants or care homes.

The book follows a journey through various areas of Shirley, Addington, New Addington and Coombe. Only the sections of Ham, Monks Orchard and Spring Park follow a chronological sequence.

The history of Shirley and Addington can still be traced by footpaths, road layout, a pub or street name, or a group of trees. Even a drain cover in the garden can give a clue to the area's past. This book is for those who want to find out and explore how their community came to be, whether they are a long-standing resident or a newcomer.

Raymond Wheeler
2002

One

Shirley Park

Shirley House from a print dated 1818 drawn by J.P. Neale, illustrating the house built by John Claxton in 1721. Previous to this there had been a house on this site recorded as 'John Best's brick messuage' and was in existence prior to 1680. Best was an embroiderer of the City of London. John Claxton's grandson, also named John, sold Shirley House to John Maberly in 1812, who spent a considerable sum of money on improvements to the property and grounds.

The road from West Wickham to Croydon ran just past Shirley House to the south, so in 1816 Maberly went to the expense of re-routing it to the north, and creating two road junctions where the roundabouts are today. Maberly's ruse to obtain permission to change the road by causing a traffic jam of farmers' dung-carts when local magnates were due to arrive for dinner with Maberly is described in J.C. Anderson's *A Short Chronicle Concerning the Parish of Croydon* (1882). John Maberly was declared bankrupt in January 1832 and his estates around Shirley were auctioned in 1834.

Shirley House seen from across the lake. In 1839 a long association with the Scott family began. The second Lord Eldon, John Scott, bought Shirley House in 1839, having lived nearby at Shirley Cottage. He had inherited the title from his grandfather, the first Lord Eldon, whose title had been conferred on him by King George III in recognition for 'Legal services' to the Crown. Shirley House remained in the possession of the Scott family until the third Lord Eldon sold the property in 1908.

The entrance gates and lodge to the Shirley Park Hotel on 21 October 1953. The entrance to Trinity school is on the same site.

By 1914 Shirley House had become the Shirley Park Hotel with a golf course and lawn tennis club. An extension to the hotel was constructed in 1935 matching the architectural style of the original house. During the First World War the hotel was used as a convalescent hospital for RAF officers. Shirley Park Hotel was demolished in 1962 and the new Trinity school built on the site. The school's previous building had been in North End, Croydon.

This photograph was taken by the main gate leading to Shirley House and looking towards the junction of Addiscombe Road and Shirley Road. The signpost is pointing westwards towards Croydon. The horse-drawn vehicle is a Croydon Corporation water cart used to damp down the dusty road surfaces during dry weather.

The upper lodge of the Eldon estate at Shirley House on 18 May 1908. This thatched dwelling was situated near the entrance to Oaks Lane. As part of the conditions for the diversion of the Wickham Road, John Maberly was required to construct a new road, namely Oaks Road. Oaks Lane ceased to become a public right of way. It is a permissive path instead.

Shirley Park Golf Club opened in 1914, part of the sports facilities of the Shirley Park Hotel. The golf course had been designed by Fowler & Simpson. The players in the first professional tournament which took place on the opening of the course were, from left to right: A. Herd, C.O. Hezlet, J.H. Taylor and C.B. Macfarlane. Born in 1871 John Henry Taylor became one of the great golfing legends before the First World War, winning the Open Championship five times. He died in 1963 at the age of ninety-one.

J.H. Taylor making the first drive in the professional competition at Shirley Park.

Sid Parker was a well-known figure in the golfing world, being a professional golfer at Shirley Park from 1944 to 1982. Before that he was assistant professional to Jimmy Wallace. He died in 2001. Having been made an honorary member after his retirement in 1982 his long association with the club totalled sixty-four years!

Looking eastward in 1926 from the junction of Addiscombe Road with Shirley Road across what was once the North Park of Shirley House. The parade of shops seen in the top photograph on page 16 was built two years later on the field in the foreground.

The 59th Battalion of the Surrey (Addington) Home Guard established themselves at the Shirley Park Hotel. In 1943 the Battalion took over the 4.5 inch anti-aircraft guns from the regular soldiers. This gun was situated at the south-west corner of the golf course in a field near to the Grimwade Avenue entrance of Lloyd Park. The tarmac road from the gate was built for the camp and still exists. Apparently it was this gun that brought down a VI flying bomb on the night of 15 June 1944, demolishing the cottages by the windmill and damaging the mill.

This view of the recently constructed Shirley Park parade of shops was taken from virtually the same position as that on page 12, but around twenty years later in 1928. The signpost by the ornamental link fencing is probably the original as seen in the earlier photograph.

With the steady increase in road traffic, a roundabout layout at the junction of Addiscombe Road and Shirley Road was deemed necessary. The completed Shirley Park roundabout scheme is seen here in 1953.

Shirley Lodge, an eighteenth-century building much altered and extended in the nineteenth century, was situated on the eastern side of Shirley Road. It was marked on John Rocque's map of Surrey (1786) and at one time its grounds extended to four acres. Shirley Lodge Farm lay to the south-east. The house consisted of three floors and a cellar with the second floor in the mansard roof. A gravel carriage drive ran round the south side of the house to the stables in the rear. One resident was John Ollis Pelton, whose father and uncle were high-class tea merchants in Croydon High Street. Pelton was chairman of Croydon Libraries Committee and took a great interest in the history of Croydon. Richard Thrale, veterinary surgeon of George Street, bought the building from Pelton. The last residents, Mr and Mrs Edwin Wade, converted the building into commercial premises in the 1930s. Shirley Lodge became the Art Silk Screen Works before being demolished in 1996, on which site Peabody's built a block of flats.

Robert Stokes took over the East Surrey Rustic Works in Stroud Green Road from his father in 1881. Here seen in this photograph taken on 28 December 1891, the business remained in the family until 1919. The houses in Glenthorne Avenue now occupy the site.

In the middle of this group of weather-boarded cottages in the hamlet of Stroud Green can be seen The Cricketers. This beer shop was opened in 1850 by George Marshall of Woodside who was a keen cricketer. Cricket was an extremely popular sport in this part of east Surrey, with a number of public houses and inns around Croydon being named after the game. The present Cricketers public house replaced the original early nineteenth-century structure in the 1920s.

The northern end of Stroud Green Road in 1908, the year it was renamed Shirley Road. The trees in the distance bordering the Lower Addiscombe Road screen Stroud Green House whose grounds later became Ashburton Park. The houses on the left were constructed in 1907 while the land on the right (formerly the Croydon Race Course) was by this time the Beckenham golf course and is now Ashburton Community school.

In 1923 Louis Paish formed Addiscombe Garden Estates Ltd to develop what became known as the Eldon estate, former lands belonging to Shirley House. In addition, Paish also developed land in Shirley Church Road and part of the Addington Palace estate. The houses in Green Court Avenue were constructed in 1927. Louis Paish's nephew was Geoff Paish, the Davis Cup tennis player.

An aerial view, taken in around 1932, showing in the foreground Valley Walk, Barnfield Avenue, and Shirley Avenue, and other roads of the Eldon estate built in 1928. Wickham Road can be seen running diagonally across this view while beyond are the fields of Spring Park Farm. The Farm Road can be seen running over the hill, as well as the newly-built houses of West Way bordering the fields in the top right-hand corner of the view.

Two
Wickham Road

The junction of Wickham Road and Shirley Road looking east in 1935. Even in 1797 Wickham Road had been described as 'an ancient highway'. In 1553 an account of the Croydon Parish boundary notes 'a highway leading from Croydon to Wickham...' The late W.J. Rowland remembered the Wickham Road's rural aspect in the early 1930s, recalling that it 'was quite a narrow thoroughfare passing through cornfields and agricultural land most of the way.'

Looking west along Wickham Road to the junction with Shirley Road, taken from the top of a bus following the No. 194 at 7.41 p.m. on 27 July 1960. On the left can be seen two items of street furniture no longer seen: the blue police box and the air-raid siren. These sirens were known as 'moaning minnies' on account of the wailing noise they emitted. The trees in the distance screened the grounds of the Shirley Park Hotel from view, while in 1962 a roundabout was created at the road junction.

Opposite above: The first recorded Methodist presence in Shirley was a Primitive Methodist chapel in the 1850s. However this did not survive long. Seventy years later the South Norwood circuit felt there was a need for a Methodist church in the Shirley area. Eventually the site was purchased in January 1926 for £1,060. The stone-laying ceremony of the new church took place on 8 July 1930 following which this notice board was erected. The first minister was Revd H. Maurice Hart who took up his duties in September 1931. This building proved to be only temporary as by 1935 a larger place of worship had been constructed and dedicated. Owing to subsidence the newer church was demolished and the present church constructed in 1997. The original church is still in use as part of the hall complex.

SHIRLEY METHODIST CHURCH
Resident Minister Rev. H. MAURICE HART.

WE HAVE BUILT THIS CHURCH FOR YOU

BUILT BY
METHODISTS FOR
ALL FREECHURCH
PEOPLE _ _ _ _

_ _ _ AND FOR
ALL WHO DO NOT
ATTEND A PLACE
OF WORSHIP.

..THIS IS THE FREE CHURCH WHICH SERVES THE DISTRICT

This part of Wickham Road was the original Shirley village. Rosemary and Myrtle Cottages are the nearest and, with the other group of cottages, date from the mid-nineteenth century. Now divided into flats, the larger building beyond the cottages was the Shirley village building dating from 1888. Opened by Alderman Frederick Edridge, within a year of its opening it was being used as a branch of Croydon Library. For many years the Shirley Working Men's Club used the ground floor while the upper floor was used for meetings and whist drives.

The meet of the Banstead drag hounds outside The Crown Inn in March 1911. At this time, The Crown was owned by Page & Overton, one of three breweries situated in Croydon in the nineteenth and early twentieth centuries. The old public house was replaced by the present building in 1937. Page & Overton's brewery was situated behind Surrey Street but note the board advertising Page & Overton's Shirley Stout (see page 54).

The lease of Shirley Cottage dated 15 May 1877 described the house as having seven bedrooms, six servants rooms, an entrance hall with covered way from the road, drawing room, dining room, library and conservatory as well as considerable grounds. Hardly warrants a name as Shirley 'Cottage'! It was built in 1721 by John Claxton in a similar style to the original Shirley House. Once the residence of Admiral Lord Radstock who fought at the Battle of St Vincent in 1797, it was here that Matthew Farrer, later the first vicar of Shirley, was born in 1816. Matthew's father was James Farrer, Master in Chancery in the early nineteenth century and step-father to Viscount Encombe who lived here prior to buying Shirley House in 1839 and before inheriting his grandfather's title as 2nd Lord Eldon. After various successive occupiers Shirley Cottage was bought by Bruce Johnson in 1932. Having lain derelict for some time, Mr Johnson restored it and converted it into six flats. Threatened with demolition in 1982, Shirley Cottage was restored again and work has recently been carried out on the property. The separate building to the east was added in 1932.

Opposite below: The nursery in Wickham Road was established in 1862 by Henry Coppin. On his death in 1885 the nursery was acquired by Thomas Butcher, whose name it carried for many years – as seen here in 1935 shortly before demolition when Wickham Road was widened. The garden centre is now part of the Wyevale Country Gardens group. The adjacent nursery business belonging to Ivall Brothers became Nursery Avenue and Nursery Close. Butchers also owned a florist shop on the corner of Wellesley Road and George Street, Croydon.

Next door to Shirley Cottage is the Shirley Parish Hall, the front section of which was once the coach house and stable block to Shirley Cottage. The new main hall, opened in 1930, was built attached at the rear in the former enclosed kitchen garden of the house. An inn, known as the Old Shirley Inn, occupied this site before the stable block was constructed.

The old village building was too small for the social functions of a growing population. The vicar of Shirley Parish church initiated various fundraising events including a Grand Bazaar in 1927 held at the Croydon Public Halls. The formal opening of the Shirley Parish Hall took place on 3 December 1930. Many groups have met here over the years including the Shirley Afternoon Townswomen's Guild, here celebrating their twenty-first anniversary on 4 June 1965.

Wickham Road in the winter of 1908. The Shirley Inn, built in 1850 and seen on the right, replaced an earlier inn of the same name on the opposite side of the Wickham Road. By 1908 the inn was a tied house of the Croydon brewery firm of Nallder & Collyer. At the time of writing Nallder & Collyer boundary plates can still be seen set in the pavement around the Shirley Inn.

The ironmonger business owned by Edgar Moyse for at least twenty-five years from 1930. The shop was situated on the corner of Barmouth Road and Wickham Road, here seen in 1932. Note the merchandise on the pavement and the advertisement billboards typical of the period. It is now a kebab shop.

The entrance lodge to Shirley Lodge Farm, also referred to as Goddard's Farm, named after Thomas Goddard who farmed here from 1880. The 1881 Census describes Thomas, aged forty-two, as a farmer of 60 acres employing three men and one boy. Ownership can be traced back to at least 1698 when the land was owned by Thomas Lockington and let to W. Thomson and W. Goldwell. The lodge stood approximately on the site of the house at the entrance to Shirley Oaks Road. It was pulled down to make way for the development of Shirley Oaks Children's Home. Mrs Edwards is seen at the doorway.

An aerial view of Shirley Oaks Children's Home taken in 1924. After protracted negotiations with Thomas Goddard, the Bermondsey Board of Guardians bought Shirley Lodge Farm in 1900 for the establishment of their children's home for the education and training of orphans and other children in the care of the St Olave's Union in Bermondsey. Children were accommodated in thirty-eight cottage homes each named after a plant, flower or tree for about sixteen children each with a housemother in charge. On site were technical training workshops, laundry buildings, a water pumping station and tower as well as a swimming pool and school. The official opening took place on 4 June 1904. By 1906 there were 609 children at the Home. Control of the Home passed to the London County Council in March 1930. Following the creation of the Greater London Council responsibility of Shirley Oaks Children's Home was given to the London Borough of Lambeth.

Opposite below: The entrance to Shirley Oaks Children's Home in Wickham Road in the 1930s. Note the ornate lanterns on the brick gateposts.

The tailoring workshop, 1907. Boys were taught a trade in tailoring, shoemaking, carpentry, plumbing or engineering. As an apprenticeship was essential for future employment care was normally taken with whom the boys would be placed. Mr R. Mansell, the building contractor, was one of a number of employers impressed by the youngsters they took on from the home.

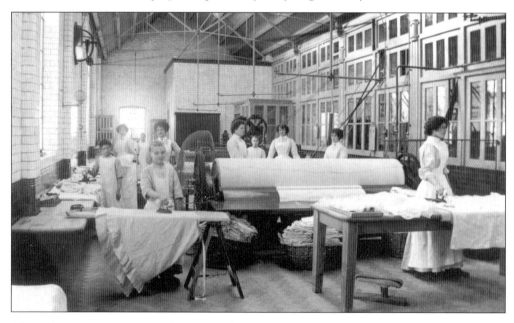

The girls practise ironing and pressing, 1907. Most girls entered service upon leaving the children's home, being supplied with a regulation serge dress, upper petticoat, under petticoat, combinations and a series of aprons for different kinds of work. These would not become their own property until a year's service had been completed.

The children enjoyed special outings and laid on entertainment. For Christmas 1908 there was an evening entertainment consisting of dances and songs including *Welcome Song*.

The children perform and sing *Little Girlies from Japan*. Following this, Christmas entertainment became a regular feature and visits to the pantomime in Croydon were regularly arranged.

Children playing outside Laburnum Cottage in 1949. Most of the cottage homes were built in pairs but a number were single units such as this. To the left the water tower and swimming pool can be seen. Lambeth's decision to close the Home instigated a long battle between Lambeth and Croydon as to the site's future development. Closure took place in July 1982. Eventually the housing estate known as Shirley Oaks Village was built and, like the school, the various roads were named after plants and flowers. A number of the cottage homes were retained and converted to flats or maisonettes. Shirley Oaks Hospital was erected on the site of the primary school which burnt down on 5 November 1982. A commemorative plaque is affixed to the surviving wall near the turning into Shirley Oaks Village. (Gerry Coll and Jad Adams have written a comprehensive history of the schools under the title A *History of Shirley Oaks Children's Home*, Deptford Forum Publishing.)

Opposite below: The first library in Shirley was established in the Shirley village building in 1888. However by the 1930s this library was becoming inadequate for the rapidly expanding population of the district. A site became vacant on the corner of Hartland Way and Wickham Road and so on 11 December 1937 a new library building was opened with due ceremony by Dr Sandison, chairman of Croydon's Libraries Committee.

Shops in the Wickham Road in 1956. The scene has altered little in over forty years, although the ornate streetlights and ownership of the shops have changed. The shop on the right is still a chemist, the Westminster Bank has closed but the Co-op next door is still there while the BP petrol station is now owned by Esso. The trees in the distance were cut down in the 1960s to make way for a new shopping parade up to Orchard Avenue.

The variety of house styles in Wickham Road is evidence of the diverse ownership of the building plots of land fronting the road. The houses on the left of this photograph taken in 1934 are in course of completion by Parmiter's. On the right is the future site of the maisonettes on the Parkfields estate, built in 1939. What became the eastern extension of Cheston Avenue was the entrance to Parkfields sports ground.

Members of the Shirley Methodist Tennis Club at Parkfields sports ground, c. 1935. From left to right are Mr and Mrs Baldwin and family, Joyce Gadd, Paddy Smith, Mrs S.G. Smith, Edgar Philpot, Nancy Lock, Mr Gidley, and Winnie Dunk, the others unknown.

Built in 1935 the Shirley Poppy public house in Wickham Road – seen here shortly after opening – took its name from Shirley's well-known breed of poppy propagated by Revd William Wilks, one time vicar of Shirley. The licence for the pub was transferred from the Surrey Arms in Cherry Orchard Road. Now a McDonalds fast-food restaurant, the original pub sign is on display inside together with a panel featuring the history of the Shirley Poppy's connections with the Revd Wilks.

A number of social and sports activities were attached to the Shirley Poppy public house including the Shirley Wanderers Rugby Club whose first season was in 1956-57. By 1961 the Wanderers acquired a clubhouse off Addington Village Road near Kent Gate. The 1st XV in 1962 taken at Sparrows Den included from left to right, back row: David Rowe, Dennis Maher, John Schofield, Chris Lane, Peter Hawkins, John Pound, John Bowles, Peter Barford-Preston. Front row: Peter Clark, Terry Cavey, Ewan Kellas, David Hunt (captain), John Marston, Dai Harvey, and John McKenzie.

Bridle Road is an ancient route once known as Coldharbour Lane linking Monks Orchard with Addington, leading through Spring Park Woods and the area now known as Shirley Heath. Apart from the lodge at the corner with Wickham Road, house building did not commence until the early 1930s. The row of three shops, Bridle Parade, were built in 1939. Note the advertisements for cigarettes and the cigarette-dispensing machine out on the pavement.

The Blue Bird Parade in 1932. Completion of the central section of this parade of shops had to wait a further five years before occupation. George Reeves & Co, the developers of the Spring Park Estate, occupied the house on the corner of Bridle Road – now the shop and yard belonging to Seccombes the builders' merchants. The local name of this shopping parade took its name from the Blue Bird confectionery shop owned by Phyllis Delve during the 1950s and '60s.

Three
Shirley Church Road

The original name for Shirley Church Road was Blue Barn Lane, named after Blue Barn Field that lay on the northern side of the lane. This straight section of highway between Shirley Road and Spring Park Road was first laid out after the enclosure of Shirley Common. The houses on the left were built in 1925, with the building line set back from the original lane before later road widening.

The church of St John the Evangelist is known as Shirley Parish church. The first ecclesiastical building on the site was a chapel built in 1835 and shortly after the Revd Matthew Farrer, half-brother of the second Earl of Eldon, was made perpetual curate as well as vicar of Addington. The present church building was designed by Sir Gilbert Scott and consecrated by Archbishop Sumner on 3 July 1856. Full parish status was granted in 1868. Compare the openness of this view dating from about 1900 with the view today, as the church is now hardly visible from the road screened by the mature trees.

Interior of St John's church, again dating from around 1900. The stained-glass window in the chancel was destroyed and other damage occurred from the blast of a flying bomb that fell in Spring Park Road in June 1944. The clock chimes of the church are based on those at Gonville and Cauis College, Cambridge, given by Maurice Byrne in memory of his wife.

It was at Shirley Vicarage that Revd William Wilks bred the Shirley poppy. He had taken a keen interest in horticulture and was secretary of the Royal Horticultural Society during which time he turned around the society's fortunes, initiating Wisley Gardens and the Chelsea Flower Show. On his retirement Wilks moved along the road to a new house built for him, The Wilderness, now the eastern wing of Hall Grange retirement home. Although now reduced in size, the gardens established by Wilks at the wilderness are opened to the public once a year under the National Gardens Scheme.

The former Shirley Vicarage was built in 1838, on one of ten parcels of land on Shirley Common purchased by the second Earl of Eldon. After Revd Matthew Farrer, the most famous occupant was Revd William Wilks, vicar from 1880 to 1912. Although no longer a vicarage, the building has a green heritage plaque installed by Croydon Council's heritage department to commemorate Revd Wilks' residence there.

A proposal in 1928 to continue the building development on the eastern side of Spring Park Road by widening the footpath to Sandpits Road, and erecting houses on the edge of the woods skirting, was thwarted by three people, namely the vicar, Mrs Anita Wall, and George Givan. Thanks to the generosity of Mrs Wall in defraying some of the cost, Croydon Corporation purchased the Shirley Church Road Recreation Ground. Mr Givan, head of the famous linen firm who lived at Shirley Court, managed to save the woods and prevent the road from being built. The Spring Park bowling club, seen here in 1938, was established as part of sporting facilities at the Recreation Ground.

One of the earliest photographs of Shirley, taken in the late 1860s, of the Fox and Goose public house, then owned by William Dean who carried on the trade of publican and baker. William's son, also William, carried on the business as well as acting as verger and sexton at Shirley church. In 1871, William moved the bakery business to Upper Shirley. The building became a private residence and in 1880 alterations were made by the then occupant, Mr J. Burgess, who renamed the building Heath Cottage. Later it was renamed Selborne House. It was demolished in the 1930s. The cart belongs to Stevensons, grocers and provision merchants of Croydon.

St John the Evangelist church and Church Cottage, c. 1890. In order to serve the growing population of Shirley it was proposed in 1834 that a schoolroom should be built in which church services could also be held. So in a cottage at the end of a row of six, at the junction with Spring Park Road, Mrs Eliza Pestell established a Dame school. Here were the beginnings of St John's primary school.

Looking down Spring Park Road. Known at one time as Bacon Row or Church Road, the road originated in 1807 when the Trustees of the waste lands sold spare land not apportioned (following the Croydon Enclosure Act of 1797), to raise funds for Croydon's second Town Hall and Buttermarket. The pair of single storied weather-boarded cottages, known as Spring Cottages – as seen on the left of the photograph – was typical of the dwellings built soon after the road was created. The road also marked the original boundary between Croydon and Addington parishes.

Ernest King's general stores in Spring Park Road in 1910. Note the window display typical of the period with advertisements for Mazawatee tea and R. White's lemonade, produced locally in their factory at Morland Road, Woodside. After 1930 the shop became known as Spring Park Stores. The shop premises are now occupied by Plumbwiser.

Although the First World War officially ended at 11.00 a.m. on the eleventh day of the eleventh month in 1918, peace with Germany was not formally signed until 28 June 1919 under the Treaty of Versailles. This event was celebrated nationally on Saturday 19 July 1919. This photograph shows the decorations and flags put out by the residents of Spring Park Road on that day.

Shirley Church Road in 1939 seen after a heavy snowfall. The weight of the snow is dragging the telephone wires almost down to road level.

The origins of St John's primary school began at the Dame school, in the charge of Mrs Eliza Pestell in 1834. By 1870 a separate boys' school had been built and the original school room in Church Cottage enlarged for girls and infants. These were replaced with a combined building that opened at twelve o'clock on 17 September 1885. At a cost of £2,330 there were only three classrooms but no hot water or staff room and the toilets were across the playground at the rear. Eliza Pestell's daughter remained in charge of the girls and infants until her retirement in 1899.

With the rapidly increasing population, and despite the opening of Benson school, pupil numbers were very high. At 2.30 p.m. on Wednesday 26 July 1944 a V1 flying bomb fell on the infants playground and exploded. The blast completely destroyed the school building. Thankfully the children and teachers were in the air-raid shelter and no injuries occurred. For the next ten years the school was housed at Benson.

Construction of a building for St John's school finally commenced in 1953. Canon Rawlins and the head teacher, Mr Gerallt 'Gary' Lewis, can be seen here inspecting building work on 24 June of that year. The official opening of the new St John's primary school took place in June 1954. Mr Lewis had been appointed head teacher in 1951 and served for sixteen years.

St John's school harvest festival celebration in 1953 in Benson school hall.

In March 1959, St John's school netball team won the Croydon Inter-Schools Netball Championship cup by beating St Mary's, Croydon, 8-1. The winning team line-up were back row, from left to right: Pat Harding, Ruth Gordon, Janet Mattocks (games teacher), Jillian Barnes, Anne Reynolds. Front row; Wendy Budd, Rosemary Myers, Suzanne Westaway, Diane Preston.

The visit of the Secretary of State for Education, Kenneth Baker, to Shirley high school on 13 June 1986. Shirley high school, formerly Shirley secondary modern school, opened in 1955. The school grounds were once part of Shirley Common. The girls in the science lesson with the Secretary of State were Alison Hall and Emma Sedgwick.

The lodge on the corner of a track way leading into the upper fields of Spring Park Farm in 1937. This farm track still exists as the path which follows the northern edge of Foxes Wood.

Swiss Lodge in 1898. This picturesque lodge in Shirley Church Road was built as part of Archbishop William Howley's considerable improvements to the Addington Palace estate. The driveway, which now leads into Pinewoods Scout Camp, originally led down to the palace from this point. The wooden timber cladding was removed in 1963 as it was found to have dry rot. Mrs Allingham can be seen standing at the door.

Addington golf course, founded in 1914, was created on the northern portion of the Addington Palace estate. This area was once Thunderfield Common, enclosed as part of the park of Addington Palace. The designer of the golf course and first secretary of the club was John Frederick Abercromby, but the First World War delayed the opening until 1922. Abercromby also designed the Addington New Golf Club, an extension opened in 1933 on the opposite side of Shirley Church Road. This course was compulsorily purchased by Croydon Corporation during the Second World War. This area is now Shirley Heath and Shrublands estate was built on the northern portion. During the night of 6 February 1952 a disastrous fire destroyed the clubhouse, including many of the club's early records. Members of the club have included Henry Longhurst, the famous golfing writer, and P.G. Wodehouse. Addington golf course is considered to be within the top forty golf courses in the world.

Four
Upper Shirley

A rare view illustrating the houses and cottages on the eastern side of Upper Shirley Road in 1904. The large house with the tall chimney pots to the right of the wooden cottages was Hillside; one-time home of John Murton the brewer, built in the 1860s. To the right of Hillside were Fern Cottages, now Nos 110 and 112 Upper Shirley Road. Hillside was demolished in the 1930s and replaced by the present house, known as Shirley Place.

Looking south up Shirley Road in 1913. A later house built in the 1920s was named Tanglewood and when that was demolished the name was given to the new development built on the site.

Woods Cottages opposite the Surprise Inn were typical examples of the many weather-boarded cottages that existed in Shirley and surrounding district. William Blundell owned the confectionery shop at the time this photograph was taken in 1914.

Shirley windmill in 1938, a tower mill built in 1854 by Richard Alwen to replace an earlier post-mill erected in 1808 by his grandfather, William, which had been destroyed in a fire. On Richard's death ownership passed to his sister, Mrs Elizabeth Thrale, who lived opposite at Shirley Hurst (later Shirley Court). In 1892 the mill ceased working but a number of restorations over the succeeding years ensured the mill's survival. Croydon Corporation bought the mill when John Ruskin school was built in 1951. Since 1995 Shirley windmill has been opened regularly to the public.

The mill cottages erected by William Alwen in 1811. George Edwards and his wife are standing at the door in this 1920s image. The cottages were destroyed by a V1 flying bomb in 1944.

The Ferns, situated just south of the windmill, was built in 1861 for Frederick Lloyd, a parasol maker. By 1876 Lewis Lamotte was in occupation and had renamed the house Heath Court. It was renamed again – this time to Windmill House – when owned by David Bernhard. The house stood empty for a number of years before being demolished in 1951 when the property was compulsorily purchased for the building of new premises for John Ruskin school, which had been transferred from Croydon.

The remains of Alwen's farm in 1946. Land to the east of Shirley Road had once formed part of Shirley Common. Coloma Convent girls' school now occupies this site.

John Ruskin school came to a new building in Upper Shirley Road in 1951 having vacated its old premises in Tamworth Road, West Croydon. A drop in pupil numbers in Croydon meant closure for the school in 1991. However, the name was transferred to the newly-created sixth form college in Selsdon Park Road. John Ruskin school was named after the famous Victorian writer whose grandmother kept the old King's Arms in Surrey Street in Croydon. He was a frequent visitor to Lady Ashburton who lived nearby at Ashburton House in Addiscombe Road. John Ruskin's parents are buried in St John's churchyard.

W.H. Mills, besides being a local historian from whom we know much of the history of Shirley and Addington, was also an accomplished artist. He painted a number of scenes in and around Shirley. His painting of Upper Shirley, completed in 1886, features the three tall chimneys of the Shirley Brewery. Originally founded by Thomas Maynard in 1840 as the Sun Brewery, it was at first a small enterprise sending out a firkin of ale on a tiny pony cart. The business later passed to Thomas's son-in-law, John Murton, and then to his son Henry Murton. An advertisement in a Croydon newspaper in 1869 read 'Henry Murton; Ale, Porter, and bitter Beer Brewer; 10d. (XK Ale) to 1/8d. (D.stout) per gallon'. The brewery changed hands again in 1870, being taken over by Messrs Ludham & Grant who, in twenty years, built up output to a maximum of 400 barrels a week. The final owner, Nathaniel Page, closed the brewery in 1892 and joined forces with Frederick Overton of the Royal Oak Brewery in Surrey Street. The name survived with Page & Overton's Shirley Brewery in Overton's Yard behind Surrey Street in Croydon. The house in the foreground survives as No. 118 Upper Shirley Road.

The Surprise Inn lies on the west side of Upper Shirley Road and was opened in 1868, having been converted from two cottages – as is illustrated by this view of the inn dating from around 1906. The inn's name commemorates the rare sighting of the Camberwell Beauty butterfly. In 1867 this species appeared in such large numbers that it was called The Great Surprise.

Upper Shirley in 1900 looking northward down Upper Shirley Road. The shop on the right was owned by William Dean, who moved the family bakery business here in 1870 from the old Fox & Goose ale house. By 1899 John 'Jack' Dean – William's son – took over the business and continued running it until his death in the 1950s. As well as the shop, John Dean also ran the Windmill café next door where a block of maisonettes now occupies the site.

On the Revd Farrer's retirement in 1879, an ornate pump was erected in his honour on the corner of Oaks Road and unveiled with due ceremony on 4 August 1880. Following his death ten years later the fountain was rededicated in his memory. When mains water was brought to Shirley, the pump was converted into a drinking fountain. However, it was removed in the 1960s despite the dedication stating that it 'should provide water for the people of Shirley forever'!

Besides his trade as the village blacksmith in Upper Shirley, George Crosskeys also ran the Temperance tea gardens on the corner of Oaks Road. Arthur Grocock later took over the tea gardens, renaming them The Rose Tree tea gardens. The tea-rooms, catering for the many day-trippers from London attracted by the countryside around Shirley and Addington Hills, disappeared in the 1935 road-widening scheme in Upper Shirley.

The Shirley Town Band setting out from The Sandrock Hotel in a brake in around 1880. The Sandrock Hotel, built in 1867 in a corner of the old sandpits, was a favoured place for excursions from London in the nineteenth century. There were many complaints made about the rowdiness of the visitors including such behaviour as 'excess drinking, dancing in the road, courting more than one lady at a time, and wearing false noses…'. These led to the temporary suspension of the Sunday licence. Here, George Pound – leader of the band – stands under the drum to the left of the child.

The original site of Shirley Fair was situated on the former village green that existed along the Wickham Road, where Shirley Parish Hall now stands. The fair then took place in a field in Upper Shirley where the Farrer memorial fountain was later built. After Addington Hills were acquired by Croydon Corporation, the fair was allowed to take place in a clear area above The Sandrock public house. The last fair was held in March 1938.

Looking down Oaks Road in 1919. The entrance to Badgers Hole leads off to the left while in the background can be seen the open heath-clad hills – often referred to as Shirley Hills – although the correct name is Addington Hills. Following the purchase of part of Addington Hills by the Local Board of Health in 1874, Croydon Corporation acquired the remainder in three stages between 1903 and 1919. Within the last hundred years, birch and oak trees have spread over the hillside restricting the views from the summit.

Croydon Manorial Court records testify to the presence of sandpits in Shirley from early in the eighteenth century. Many of the workers settled in the hollow of the Addington Hills known as Badgers Hole, seen here in 1907. This settlement was also known as Dunk's Hollow. A beer house with the name of the Badger Inn existed here as well. The single storey wooden-clad cottages were demolished in 1935 but the other houses, including Alwens Cottages, still survive. The boundary between Croydon and Addington parishes ran through the settlement approximately where the children are standing.

Overlooking Upper Shirley from the slopes above Badgers Hole.

Looking down Shirley Hills Road in 1925. Nearly every cottage in Upper Shirley had signs advertising teas. The group of eight cottages on the left, opposite The Sandrock public house, was known as Teapot Row. These cottages were demolished ten years later in 1935 to make way for road widening.

The former mission church in October 1960. Now an attractive-looking house with a bell tower, this private residence was converted from a church-cum-school. Although part of Upper Shirley, and only a few hundred yards up the hill from The Sandrock, this building was situated in the parish of Addington. The mission school opened on 13 April 1874 under the direction of Miss Ann Marie Jarrett as schoolmistress.

The interior of the mission showing the altar and east window of the chapel.

A contrast in time and fashion from the photograph below are the children of the Addington mission school in 1907. Miss Jarrett was still in charge in 1908 when the school closed and she continued to reside nearby until her death in 1915, aged seventy-five. Miss Jarrett, seen in the back row on the left of the photograph, must have been quite a character as the hill gained the nickname Jarrett's Hill. W.H. Mills was one of its pupils.

Coloma Convent girls' school relocated in 1966 from its former site in Tavistock Road, Croydon to Upper Shirley Road on land next to Shirley Court. Shirley Court, built by Peter Thrale in 1870 and now within the school grounds, is the convent house of the Daughters of Mary and Joseph. Jane Marchini (née Coventry) – seen in the top middle row, second from the left – provided this photograph of the sixth form in 1972.

The oldest family business in Shirley was Bennett's. John Bennett came up from West Sussex in 1777 as a boy and later established a broom-making business in Wickham Road, approximately where Verdayne Avenue joins Wickham Road. By 1839 he owned twenty-five acres which he farmed. In 1888 his grandson, William, moved the broom-making business to the sandpit site at the bottom of Sandrock Road and, as seen here in 1911, branched out into building materials and horticultural products. By the 1980s Albert Bennett & Sons were using the Shirley windmill as a trademark for their products.

The Bennett family also set up a bus and coach hire business known as Shirley Coaches, garaging the firm's vehicles in Sandpits Road. Bennett's operated the first bus to New Addington in 1937. Albert Bennett is seen standing between the two Bedford pick-ups in 1938. In 1987 the business was sold and the Birkdale housing development began.

Five

Ham Farm

A painting of Ham Farm dating from 1830. The history of Ham can be traced back to the time of the Domesday Book in 1086 and Ham Farm was also mentioned in 1332 when it was known as the home of Ralph atte Ham. Later, in Archbishop Warham's survey of Croydon in 1511, the area was known as the Borough of Ham. In 1745 Peter Burrell purchased the estate, adding it to his lands held in Beckenham. Peter Burrell's grandson, also Peter Burrell, sold Ham in 1835 to Samuel Jones Loyd, who already had land at Monks Orchard.

Ham Lodge, 7 February 1960. Built in the 1840s, it stood in Wickham Road at the end of the farm drive leading to Ham Farm. The lodge once stood in half an acre of garden but lost much to modern development and was finally demolished in 1980. The remaining gatepost was removed in 1980 and for many years stood in the grounds of St George's church, but is now housed at nearby Edenham high school.

The farm road leading from Ham Lodge to Ham Farm. This is now Orchard Avenue.

The main farmhouse of Ham Farm, *c.* 1920. The original core of the building consisted of a medieval open hall timber-framed building but was rebuilt in the middle of the nineteenth century. From the Monks Orchard sales particulars of 1920 it is known that the house contained nine bedrooms, three bathrooms, a tennis lawn, stabling and coach house. Frederick Loyd's last tenant farmer at Ham was Mr Alexander Edgar. Loyd sold Ham to Percy Portway Harvey in 1920.

The farm pond. This is where animals belonging to Carmo's Circus took their bath (see page 68.)

In 1920 Percy Harvey Estates Ltd purchased the Ham Farm estate for £14,120. The company advertised the estate by stressing the rural nature of the area and envisaged purchase by smallholders rather than by building firms. The failure of the company to make any attempt at planning made for a haphazard development in the 1920s of shacks, old railway carriages and more substantial houses along the alignment of existing farm tracks that became increasingly rutted and muddy. This is typified here in this view looking north along The Glade, dating from about 1923, approximately from where Greenview Avenue was later built on the right. The bungalow in the distance is now 149 and 149A The Glade.

Monks Orchard primary school in The Glade opened in 1936 to cater for the educational needs of the families now moving into the rapidly developing area of the Ham Farm estate. In common with many schools in Croydon pupils were evacuated at the commencement of hostilities in 1939. For a while the acting head was Miss Pedgrift, who later became head of Winterbourne infants school in Thornton Heath. The author knew her as head when he attended Wintebourne infants as a small boy.

The genesis of St George's church began in April 1926 when Shirley Parish church council paid £1,250 for three acres of land together with Ham Farm Cottage. Plans to build a new church only came to fruition in 1937 when the first St George's was completed in August of that year. This is now the present church hall. The war delayed plans for the building of a permanent church building. However, construction began in November 1951 and continued through with the dedication by the Archbishop of Canterbury taking place on 15 November 1952.

Building work in progress on the new St George's church in 1952. The builders were Messrs James Longley. Construction of the Lady chapel, east end, choir gallery and vestries commenced in May 1966.

Nos 1 and 3 Woodmere Avenue under construction in 1935. Behind the houses the farmhouse is in the process of demolition. From 1925 Ham Farm became the winter quarters for Carmo's Circus. When the Great Carmo (Henry Cameron) moved his circus there he renamed the house Carmo Manor. Until 1935, when the circus tent was destroyed in a fire whilst on tour, the sounds of the jungle could be heard in this part of Shirley. Despite a few complaints about the lions and tigers the animals were popular, especially the elephant taking a bath in the old farm pond.

Improved development came to the area by the 1930s. New roads were constructed linking the estate with Woodside and Elmers End via Gladeside and Bywood Avenue. Messrs E. & L. Berg built better quality housing on the site of Lorne Poultry Farm. An ARP exercise is seen here taking place in Lorne Avenue in 1939, soon after the commencement of the Second World War. The use of poison gas by the enemy was particularly feared.

Six

Monks Orchard

The estate of Monks Orchard took its name from a field by the same name, almost certainly originating from a family name of Munke in 1552. Rocque's map of 1762 shows a farm here as West Shirley Farm, which later became Park Farm. It was once part of the Langley estate belonging to Sir Peter Burrell (Lord Gwydir) of Beckenham on whose death Park Farm was purchased by John Maberly for £6,000.

In 1833 Park Farm was purchased by Samuel Jones Loyd, an eminent nineteenth-century banker and partner in the banking company, Jones, Loyd and Co. His ideas on financial strategy became the basis of the financial system in Britain today. For his services to the nation Samuel Loyd was created Baron Overstone (named after his residence in Northamptonshire) in 1860. In 1853 Samuel Loyd sold the estate to his cousin Lewis Loyd, who built a new mansion situated to the north of Park Farm and naming it Monks Orchard. Considerable improvements were made to Monks Orchard including new entrance drives and lodges, a parterre and formal gardens, as well as enlargements of the lakes. Lewis Loyd was prominent in the community of Shirley and a great benefactor to St John's church.

On the death of Lewis Loyd in 1891 at the age of eighty, Monks Orchard passed to his nephew, Frederick Loyd. The last occupant was Arthur Gurney Preston whose brother, Edwin Mumford Preston, owned the Warren near Hayes Common and was commemorated in the name Preston's Road. In 1920 Arthur Preston tragically died in a bathing accident in Newquay. The site was eventually purchased by Bethlem Royal Hospital in 1924. Monks Orchard House is seen here across one of the three ornamental lakes linked by waterfalls. These lakes were later filled in by the hospital for safety reasons but are remembered in the name of nearby Lake Road.

The drawing room of Monks Orchard House from a photograph in the sales particulars of 1924. It stated that the room was 39ft by 24ft, handsomely decorated with a white marble mantelpiece, oak floor and gilt and white plaster ceiling.

Lewis Loyd improved his property considerably, building a Tudor style lodge at the end of the western drive on the Wickham Road. This drive later became Cheston Avenue, named after John Cheston, one of the architects of Bethlem Royal Hospital. The carved coat of arms in the gable of Tudor Lodge features those of Loyd quartered with that of his wife, Frances Irby, with Non Mihi – part of the family motto Non Mihi sed Patria – 'not for myself but for my country.'

The eastern lodge is in the style of a Greek temple and was also known variously as Classical Lodge or White Lodge. Here the gamekeeper lived and older residents have memories of rabbits hanging up outside! A similar lodge to White Lodge existed at the end of the northern drive on Upper Elmers End Road.

Bethlem Royal Hospital was founded in 1247 becoming the Priory Hospital of St Mary of Bethlehem. The name became shortened to Bethlem. The original site of the hospital is now Liverpool Street station in London. Before the hospital's relocation to Monks Orchard in 1925 it occupied the building which now houses the Imperial War Museum. The intention was to retain Monks Orchard Mansion but as extensive dry rot had been discovered it was pulled down to be replaced by the ward block, Witley House. Remains of the parterre still survive. The formal opening of Bethlem Royal Hospital took place in July 1930 by Queen Mary.

A tutorial group outside the nurses' home in 1956. The nurses' home itself, renamed Alexander House in 1980, was closed in 1994 and the building now houses offices. Female nurses began wearing uniform in 1891 but the uniform was abandoned in the 1970s.

Pond House was situated on the Shirley and West Wickham border, accessed by a little bridge over the River Bec. Originally an old coaching inn called the King's Arms, it dated back to 1753 if not earlier. In 1821 Edward Little acquired the building and renamed it Pond House, the licence passing to the weather-boarded beer house, the White Hart, across the pond. The present White Hart replaced this little building in 1908. In 1863 Pond House became part of the Monks Orchard estate. After the sale of Monks Orchard in 1924, there was a succession of owners. In 1944 it was damaged by a flying bomb and finally demolished in 1946. Crittenden Lodge and the caravan park now occupy the site.

Seven

Spring Park

The thatched cottage, believed to date from the reign of Queen Anne, was once the lodge at the entrance to the long farm road leading to Spring Park Farm. The drive continued past Spring Park House and joined the ancient lane leading to Addington, now Bridle Road. A further lodge still exists on the corner of Bridle Road, No. 792 Wickham Road. From 1921 the thatched lodge became a café but after a fire in 1968 it became the office of estate agents, R.W. Johnson & Co. now taken over by Allen Russell.

The southern aspect of Spring Park House looked out onto lawns and a lake. The house, first known as Coldharbour, possibly dated from the early eighteenth century and, according to the deeds of Addington Place estate, the house was tenanted from 1768 by Arthur Chichester, fifth Earl of Donegal. The most noteworthy occupant was Hewitt Davis, a forerunner in developing modern farming techniques who transformed the property and adjoining farm, Coldharbour, from a 'rabbit warren' of boggy, gravelly soil into Spring Park, a model farm attracting visitors from afar. Later occupants included Sydney Stebbing and his second wife, Amy Chamberlain, the daughter of Walter Chamberlain, mayor of Croydon from 1927 to 1929. From 1953 Spring Park House was used as a nurses home for those working at Bethlem Royal Hospital. Spring Park House was finally demolished in 1963.

Following the break up of the Monks Orchard estate in 1924, Spring Park Farm was purchased by Samuel Worksett of Chislehurst for £7,000. In 1929 he sold the estate for £15,000 to Alfred Temple Bennett, James Oswald and Herbert Ferris Worskett, the son of Samuel. Alfred Temple Bennett was an engineer by profession, manufacturing automatic fog signals for Trinity House in 1902 as well as producing aircraft parts during the First World War. In 1922 he diversified into 'pirate' bus operations running vehicles under the Admiral name from Wood Green to Winchmore Hill in north London. Within the family concerns were a coal merchants business, which his father first began, and a taxi firm. Alfred Temple Bennett was an active freemason, a Justice of the Peace for the County of Middlesex and he became Deputy Chair of Edmonton Petty Sessional Division in 1950. He died in May 1969 at Winchmore Hill.

Opposite below: Ralph Stebbing married Margaret Aston at St John's church, Shirley, on 20 August 1938. The wedding party is photographed on a punt in the middle of the main lake, now in private ownership. During the Second World War, Ralph served as a Lieutenant in the Royal Artillery but tragically was killed in action in Malaya in January 1942. The stained-glass window in the Lady Chapel of All Saints church was given by Sydney Stebbing in memory of his son, Ralph.

An aerial view looking north and taken in 1935 of the western half of the Spring Park Farm estate, developed by Alfred Temple Bennett and his partners. James Oswald died in 1932 so Bennett's son, Stuart Morris Bennett, joined the partnership in his place. The three partners, Alfred Temple Bennett, Stuart Morris Bennett and Herbert Ferris Worskett, then formed the company Gower Builders (London) Ltd. The road at the bottom of the photograph is South Way. To the right, the southern half of Temple Avenue can be seen, but the northern section of this road had yet to be built, likewise the eastern half of Bennetts Way. The triangular space in the foreground is the future site of Benson school. Foxes Wood is seen in the bottom of the view.

The houses in West Way together with a few in Bennetts Way were constructed by Brown Brothers in 1932. However within a year or so they had gone out of business. To continue the development John G. Cronk & Son Ltd, well-known builders in south and south-west London, were contracted to build houses in East Way, Bennetts Way and a few in South Way.

South Way in 1935. This particular road has houses built by Browns, and Cronks, as well as Gower Builders. Evidence of the builders' names can be seen in many of the older drain covers still in situ in the driveways of houses in Spring Park.

C TYPE   **£855 FREEHOLD**

3 Bedroom Type

£45 Total Deposit   **Weekly repayments 24s.**

No Road Charges, Legal Fees, or Stamp Duties

Solid drawn copper tubes throughout. General fittings include chromium plated door furniture, switches, etc., throughout. Lighting points to holders in all rooms, also porch and boxroom. Six power points. Tiled surrounds. Gas points in all main rooms. Overmantels, fireplaces and decorations to choice of Purchaser.

Development of the eastern half of the estate began from 1935, marketing the distinctive style of semi-detached houses under the designs of Gower A, B, C, D, and E. Other designs included detached properties with further letter codes. Here is the design of a Gower B taken from the sales catalogue of 1935. The houses are still known by their letter designs by local estate agents.

The Bennett consortium did not have a complete monopoly of the development of the Spring Park Farm estate. Another Spring Park developer was Sydney John Hunt. He was born in April 1898 and brought up in South Norwood. During the 1920s he worked for Wylie & Berlyn Ltd, another Shirley developer, but in the spring of 1933 he commenced house building in Hartland Way beginning from Shirley Church Road end and continuing downhill. Each house was to have a name commencing with the letter A and working through the alphabet. Sydney Hunt is here seen on the right of the photograph. In 1937 he built his own house Cornerways on the corner of Shirley Church Road. During the Second World War Sydney Hunt joined the RAF and commanded 5014 Squadron, a Works squadron specialising in the repair of war-damaged airfields in the UK and in Europe.

By 1937 Hunt had completed houses in Langland Gardens and Devonshire Way with three types of houses advertised for sale namely the 'Triple-eight' semi-detached at £888, the 'Triple-nine' detached priced at £999 and the 'Ten-twenty', a four-bed detached at £1,020. Intended purchasers could have the luxury of 'Chillproof' central heating at extra cost. Sydney Hunt with the Mayor of Croydon, Alderman A. Peters, at the formal opening of one of the houses. After the war Sydney Hunt returned to building in Langland Gardens and Wickham Road before opening his own estate agency business. He died in 1959.

On the evening of 19 September 1940, a parachute mine was dropped on Langland Gardens. Three members of the Jarvis family were killed at No. 1, as were members of the Lansman family at No. 5. Nos 1, 3, 5 and 7 were completely demolished while others in the road were severely damaged. Parachute mines were dropped in pairs but the second mine, which fell in Addisons Close, failed to explode.

As with the rest of Croydon, Shirley had its own share of V1 flying bombs. On 26 June 1944 a flying bomb damaged houses in Shirley Way. Here a policeman is standing guard outside the damaged houses.

In common with the rest of the country, Shirley residents had to endure the hardships caused by the war. After a night spent in air-raid shelters, Shirley commuters faced the task of reaching work with the difficulties of dislocated transport. In the evenings many served in the ARP or Home Guard. Those whose homes were damaged may have spent the night in the rest centre at Shirley Parish Hall. The voluntary organisations worked tirelessly, including the Salvation Army who set up their mobile canteen in Shirley Way offering refreshments to those forced out of their homes and to the men from the rescue squads.

All Saints church, a Grade II listed building since 1998, was built in 1956, being partly funded by proceeds from a war-damaged church in Canterbury that was never rebuilt. As Spring Park, part of Addington Parish, began to develop throughout the 1930s it was realised that the area needed a church of its own. Land was purchased on the corner of Bridle Road and the main drive to Spring Park House but the war delayed building work. Eventually, on 24 January 1948, two ex-RAF huts were dedicated as a temporary church. The architect was William Curtis Green (1875-1960) whose other Croydon designs included St George's church, Waddon. All Saints church was consecrated by the Archbishop of Canterbury, the Right Revd Dr Geoffrey Fisher, on 9 December 1956.

The churches in the area provided the base for many voluntary groups and social activities. Spring Park Dramatic Club is a well-known repertory group in Shirley using the church hall built in 1952, as its venue. Here, members of All Saints are performing in the Sunday school pantomime in 1956.

The 7th Shirley (All Saints) Guides Company was founded in 1952 and celebrated their Golden Jubilee in 2002. The girls had their photograph taken in the playground of Spring Park infant's school in 1955. The infants school facing Bridle Road opened on 31 August 1954 as a response to the rapid expansion of the school originally opened in 1949. Both infants and junior departments merged to form one school in 1998.

The area now occupied by Shrublands was once part of a large tract of woodland known as Spring Park Wood. The southern section later became the Addington New Golf Course. However, in 1946 Croydon Corporation made a compulsory purchase order for the golf course to relieve the severe housing shortage after the war and temporary accommodation in the form of prefabricated housing was erected. By 1961 plans had been drawn up to replace the prefabs, and the communal grassed areas between the new houses, flats and maisonettes were intended to create a semi-rural atmosphere.

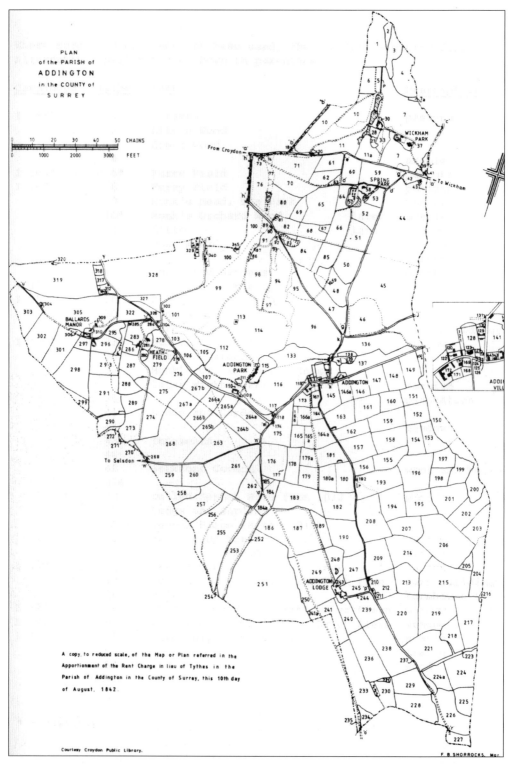

Addington Tithe Map, dated 1842, redrawn to a reduced scale by F.B. Shorrocks in 1983.

Eight
Addington

In 1768 Alderman Barlow Trecothick, who was Lord Mayor of London for a few months in 1770, bought the Addington estate for £38,500 from Anne Spencer. He began to plan for a new mansion, Addington Place, a quarter of a mile to the west of the original Leigh manor house situated north of St Mary's church. The architect appointed was Robert Mylne. Barlow Trecothick died in 1775 but before his death he insisted his nephew and heir, James Ivers, take the name of Trecothick. Mylne was retained and they completed the Palladian-style building in 1778. Built of Portland stone Addington Place consisted of a two-storied central block with on each side single-storey wings terminating in gabled-ended pavilions. On completion of the new building, the old house was demolished. James Trecothick then commissioned Lancelot 'Capability' Brown for 'improvements', as his landscaping was known. The park today still contains features of his work.

In 1807 Trecothick's mansion was purchased for the Archbishop of Canterbury using finance from the sale of the old Archbishops' palace in Croydon. Addington Place now became Addington Palace. The most significant changes were undertaken by Archbishop William Howley (1828-1848). The height of the wings were increased to two storeys bringing them level with the main building. Four new lodges were erected at the entrances to the estate. Of these only the south lodge at the entrance to the public park in Kent Gate Way and the stable lodge remain in their original condition. Swiss Lodge was substantially renovated in 1963 (see page 47).

In 1898 Frederick English, a South African diamond millionaire, bought Addington Palace. He employed the eminent architect Richard Norman Shaw to restructure the house, restoring the original outline of the building and creating the salon with its chandelier. English died in 1909 and Mrs English refused to sleep there again, returning to South Africa. During the First World War Addington Palace was used as a military hospital for cases of enteric fever and malaria. The cars in the photograph, from left to right, are an Austin, a Siddeley-Deasy and a Rover.

Many of the troops who were treated at Addington Palace had seen service in India, Mesopotamia, and the Far East. A number of huts were erected across the park to the north in the vicinity of what is now Bishop's Walk, providing temporary ward accommodation.

Staff at dinner in the Addington Palace War Hospital in 1915. Ten years after the First World War, part of the park was sold to Croydon Corporation as a public park and the remainder leased to the Addington Palace Golf Club, with the Palace used as the club house.

Convalescing soldiers in the grounds of Addington Palace. Many of the trees planted by 'Capability' Brown to screen the house from the road, mainly beech with ash and chestnut, can still be seen. He may also have planted the Great Cedar of Lebanon tree on the rear lawn. It is one of the largest cedars in Britain and has a commemorative plaque as one of the 'great trees of London'.

From 1953 Addington Palace became home to the Royal School of Church Music. A number of organs were installed in the rooms of the Palace. The winter garden, in use for a while as a locker room for the golf club, was converted into a chapel. After forty-three years, the RSCM were unable to afford the upkeep of the building so in 1996 moved to smaller premises near Dorking. Addington Palace, now a country club owned by the Westmead Group, is opened to the public on a regular basis. Civil weddings take place in the former chapel.

Looking down Spout Hill with Lion Lodges on the right. Lion Lodges were built 1778-79, part of the rebuilding scheme of Addington Place. The lions refer to those in the Arms of the Leigh family. An avenue of lime trees lined the drive from the lodges to the main house. In 1780 Trecothick harnessed the water from a spring above the lodges by building a water spot in the form of a lion's head. In 1844 pipes were laid to connect the Spout Hill spring with the village below. In 2002 some residents still had free water rights.

Addington Parish church, dedicated to St Mary the Virgin, from a print dated 1820. The present church dates from around 1080 when the nave and chancel were built. The original tower, as seen in this print, was built in the twelfth century while the south aisle was added in 1210. The porch was added in 1843 and incorporated the initials of Archbishop Howley. Further alterations were made in 1876 when the tower was raised a second time and the north aisle added. St Mary's contains a number of monuments inside including an impressive monument to the Leigh family in alabaster and black Sussex marble.

From the same angle as the view above, this photograph of the church and the cottages in the village road dates from 1892. The pair of cottages next to the church was demolished while the pair of cottages next to the churchyard was demolished around 1910 when the area was added to the graveyard. Note also the penny-farthing bicycles.

The twenty-feet-high cross presented and dedicated by Archbishop Randall Davidson in 1911. It was erected in memory of the five Archbishops of Canterbury buried in Addington, namely: Charles Manners Sutton, William Howley, John Bird Sumner, Charles Thomas Longley and Archibald Campbell Tait.

What is now known as the Old Vicarage was built in 1867 and stands to the north of Addington Village Road, separated from Addington House by the cricket ground. The vicarage served the parish for nearly one hundred years until the smaller one was built at the foot of Spout Hill in 1956. It is believed the original vicarage stood to the south of The Cricketers Inn.

Revd Frederick Nixon was vicar of Addington from 1925 to 1938. His sister, Miss May Nixon, is standing at the door of the vicarage in 1927. With her are Mr and Mrs Horner and the maid.

Addington National school in 1900. Built by Archbishop Howley in 1844 on the corner of Spout Hill, the school building replaced two cottages known as the Workhouse in which, in 1794, was established the first Addington school. The children came to the school from the village and surrounding districts, including Sanderstead, Monks Orchard and Layhams. When snow began to fall the children would be sent home in case the lanes became impassable.

Addington National school in the 1920s. The school closed on 30 January 1950 with the pupils transferring to Wolsey primary school or the newly built Gilbert Scott school. Elsie Nina Foster, formerly head teacher of the village school from 1938, became the first head of Gilbert Scott before finally retiring in 1968. After closure the school building was used as a parish hall for a time but was finally demolished in 1967. The site of the school is now an open green.

Addington Village Road, seen from the western end, c. 1910. In the centre are the buildings of Lower Farm now replaced by the electricity sub-station and the police station. Lower Farm was acquired by Henry Still in 1867. Each farm in Addington had its own pond whilst a much larger one existed behind where the photographer was standing.

Even as late as the 1950s Addington still retained its rural atmosphere. The village shop was offering teas to cyclists and motorists. Behind the shop is the turning into Lodge Lane although by this time a short by-pass had been constructed allowing buses and other vehicles to New Addington to avoid the village.

Opposite The Cricketers Inn (now the Addington Village Inn) was the Home Farm of the Addington Palace estate. On Bonfire Day 1877 a fire destroyed much of the farm and surrounding buildings but these were rebuilt. The long stable building was renovated in the early 1970s.

Addington House, now in Boundary Way, was the farmhouse to Upper Farm (also known as Addington Park Farm). It is a medieval hall house originally consisting of a 2-bay open hall with a cross passage and storerooms in the north. Further extensions were made in the seventeenth century and a major extension of the 1790s forms an 'L' around the original buildings. Addington House had been in the hands of the Still family for three generations. In 1867 Henry Still of Chelsham acquired the leases of both Upper and Lower Farms. Both Henry and his son, William H. Still, were almost 'squires' of the village. When the late Lilian Thornhill conducted a survey of Addington House in 1978, Miss Kathleen Still, granddaughter of Henry Still, was the owner.

There was just one shop in the village, which opened in October 1881 as a co-operative enterprise with 250 shares at five shillings each and the remainder at two shillings and sixpence. From 1884 it also served as the post office. By 1906, the date of this photograph, the shop had become a haven for ramblers and cyclists by selling refreshments. The eastern half of the building contained the home for a curate. Post office facilities were transferred to the parade of shops in Selsdon Park Road in the 1960s and the shop closed soon after. Peter Cairns bailiff to William Still is seen on horseback.

The Victorian novelist R.S. Surtess once referred to the local hunting scene around Croydon in his book *Jorrocks' Jaunts and Jollities*. This view of a meet of the Old Surrey Hounds outside The Cricketers Inn dates from 1910. The inn was erected in 1844 replacing a much more ancient inn named The Three Lions, a reference to the arms of the Leigh family, which stood behind the Victorian building. The name 'Cricketers' may have originated from the formation of the first Addington Cricket Club in 1743.

Addington cricket team of 1885. Addington Cricket Club can claim to be the oldest cricket club in the country having been formed in 1743 when in that year an XI from Addington played the London Cricket Club at the Honourable Artillery Company's ground at Finsbury. Cricket was played on part of Long Meadow, now the front garden of the Old Vicarage. The pitch was maintained by William 'Bonker' Coppin, parish constable and clerk. Having been born with a clubfoot he earned the nickname 'bonker' from the sound he made when walking. The nickname is remembered in the Bunker's Knob pub in Fieldway.

Participants in the annual race on 8 April 1910 in which the Addington Park estate workers took part in the 4-mile course. W.H. Mills recorded the names. From left to right are: J. Smith (Gardener), ? Turner (Butler), Batchelor (secretary), Williams (footman), ? Davis, Henry ? , Shurman (coachman), Herbert Boatwright, ? Mills (gardener), Percy Alexander, Fred Mills (gardener), and Harry ? (gardener). Williams the footman, who completed the run in twenty-three and half minutes, won a silver-plated biscuit barrel.

The village smithy in Addington is probably well over three hundred years old. The Coppin family served as blacksmiths for many years, with Leslie Coppin being the last member to follow his ancestors as blacksmith in the early years of the twentieth century.

On 29 January 1885 the sinking of a well in the chalk at Hares Bank in Featherbed Lane commenced. Work took some time and the pumping station eventually opened on 2 August 1888. One and a half million gallons of water a day, raised by two beam engines, were produced after opening. The first engine built by Easton & Anderson was installed in 1888, and the second engine built by Glenfield & Kennedy of Kilmarnock installed in 1893. Reconstruction of the pumping station took place in the 1970s and the old building was demolished in 1976. The engines are now in museums.

Nine

New Addington

View looking south towards the downs and the fields belonging to Castle Hill Farm, *c.* 1920. The future estate of New Addington would be built fifteen years later.

Lodge Lane leading from the village to Castle Hill and Addington Lodge Farm in the 1930s. Addington was one of the last areas of Croydon to lose its rural aspect.

William H. Still acquired Castle Hill Farm in 1889 from Lennard of Wickham Court. It stood in Lodge Lane just north of the entrance to Headley Drive. The name Castle Hill is traditionally linked with the legendary castle of Baron Robert Aguillon who lived in Addington in 1270-71. Opposite the farmhouse was a field known as Mill Field, possibly the site of a windmill which is believed to have existed there. The land on which the first estate of New Addington was built was purchased from W. H. Still in the 1930s.

After the Second World War New Addington began to expand rapidly, yet for many years Lodge Lane remained a fairly narrow road with insufficient room for the tractor and bus to pass with ease. The 130 bus commenced operation from Croydon to Salcot Crescent on 5 July 1939. In 1952 the route was extended to a new terminus in Homestead Way. The 130 route, under threat following construction of Tramlink, was granted a reprieve.

Addington Lodge Farm stood in a very isolated position on the ridge overlooking Featherbed Lane at a height over 500 feet. In 1581, Sir Olliphe Leigh of Addington Place made a will in which he 'granted to Sir John Leigh of Eastwickham, Kent, and William Lynterne of Thorpe, Surrey, all his farme house called Addington Lodge and all houses edifices' in Addington and Farleigh. In 1802 when the whole of Addington Parish was auctioned Addington Lodge was the largest farm, totalling 720 acres.

A haycart crossing one of the fields of Addington Lodge Farm. In 1914 the farm was purchased by a Mr Fisher of Sidcup and from then on it became known as Fisher's Farm. The farmhouse, although damaged by fire in 1938, still survives as a Croydon Council depot and recycling centre.

Building commenced in New Addington in 1935 when the First National Housing Trust, founded by Charles Boot, purchased 569 acres of Addington Lodge Farm for the creation of 'New Addington Garden City' where 'workpeople can enjoy the beauty of the countryside'. The original intention of building 4,400 houses on the site never materialised as the Second World War interrupted the project, by which time only a quarter of the houses had been constructed. After the war all subsequent development was in the hands of Croydon Corporation.

King Henry's Drive under construction in July 1953. Between 1949 and 1955 the development of New Addington proceeded apace with the Corporation offering tenders to a number of construction firms. The overall effect appeared to be of a haphazard development which attracted local opposition at the time. However for most residents the housing was far superior from which they had moved. The coach in the background probably belongs to Worrell's Coaches.

With 55,000 people on Croydon's housing waiting list after the war, the need to provide housing quickly resulted in the compulsory purchase of the undeveloped land belonging to the First National Housing Trust. Some 320 prefabricated houses erected at Castle Hill for homeless families with young children were occupied from three years after the war as seen here in 1956.

The Addington Hotel was built in 1937 on the corner of King Henry's Drive. It was renamed The Cunningham in 1981 after fighter pilot John 'Cat's Eyes' Cunningham. The first pilot to shoot down an enemy aeroplane using radar during the Second World War, Cunningham was highly decorated for his war service. He died in July 2002 aged eighty-four.

The new estate at New Addington was quite remote, being five miles from Croydon. At first there were no public transport links until March 1938 when a bus service, operated by A. Bennett & Sons of Shirley, commenced linking New Addington with route 64 at Featherbed Lane. Their bus is seen here behind Central Parade in 1938. The route operated until July 1939 when London Transport's route 130 commenced operation.

The first building for public worship consisted of two ex-Army huts joined together and erected in 1946 on land offered to the Diocesan authorities by W.H. Still. This church, dedicated to St George, was situated at the junction of Lodge Lane and King Henry's Drive but unfortunately was destroyed in a fire on 12 March 1958. Today a block of flats stands on the site opposite the Cunningham Pub. Members of St George's congregation held a Family Week in January 1952.

In 1950 Croydon Corporation, who had assumed responsibility for the development of New Addington, allocated a three-acre site at the top of Central Parade for church use. Plans were made to build a parish hall, vicarage and permanent church building with Caroe & Partners appointed as architects. The foundation stone for the new St Edward's church was laid by the Bishop of Croydon, Rt Revd John Hughes. Archbishop Geoffrey Fisher consecrated the completed church on 8 October 1958.

An aerial view looking beyond St Edward's church to Milne Park. In 1930 an application was made for the use of a field belonging to Addington Lodge Farm as a private aerodrome. Croydon Corporation objections were overruled by the Ministry of Health. In 1933 the British Hospital Air pageant, organised by C.W.A. Scott, was held at the aerodrome featuring aerobatics, parachute jumping and wing-walking. British Air Transport, who founded the aerodrome, eventually moved to Gatwick in 1944. The land was acquired for housing but it was declared green belt land in 1963. Milne Park, the remaining part of this former airfield, forms part of a chain of open spaces that runs from one end of New Addington to the other.

New Addington market on 22 June 1973. The twice-weekly market continues to be well patronised and in addition the North East Surrey Farmers' Market group commenced a monthly market in Central Parade in 2002.

In 1949 the government agreed that a limited amount of industry was essential to the development of New Addington. As a result the Vulcan Way industrial estate was established with, due to planning regulations, predominantly light engineering firms. By 1954, twenty-one firms were employing 2,000 people. One of the companies was the automotive chemical company, Douglas Holt Ltd. This company pioneered oven-cleaning spray aerosols in 1965.

The first permanent school in New Addington was Overbury, which opened in July 1939. With the rapidly expanding estate, a further school became essential. Wolsey junior school, in King Henry's Drive, opened its doors in 1949 while the infants department opened two years later in April 1951.

The original Fairchildes school building dating from 1869, believed to have been built by the then owner of the Fairchildes estate just over the southernmost border of Addington Parish. The first log book indicated there were two teachers at the school in 1879. On closure of the school in 1951 most of the pupils were transferred to Biggin Hill while others relocated to the present Fairchildes primary school built in the same year.

New Addington suffered its share of bombing during the Second World War. A V1 flying bomb caused this damage to recently constructed houses in Gascoigne Avenue during the night of 28/29 June 1944.

Fieldway under construction. As a consequence of the post-war 'baby boom' Croydon Corporation applied for and was granted permission to develop 87 acres north of Dunley Drive in 1963. The construction contract was awarded to John Laing Construction Co. Ltd who completed the estate, with its shops, schools and 1,412 houses, by February 1968. Only two blocks of flats were built instead of the seven originally envisaged.

Ten

The Road to Coombe

A contrast to today's busy dual carriageway, Gravel Hill was once a country lane, as seen here on 8 September 1934. The signpost by the kissing gate indicates a footpath leading across the fields of the Heathfield estate to Selsdon. There is no trace of the path today. Gravel Hill tram stop is now on the right.

Heathfield House, at the top of Gravel Hill, was once the farmhouse of Stones Farm, listed as a sheep farm in the 1802 sale of the Addington estate. The name Heathfield dates from 1837 when it appears on the tithe assessment for Addington Parish. In 1872 Henry Goschen occupied Heathfield. The main drive originally crossed the fields from half way up Gravel Hill but Henry virtually rebuilt the late eighteenth-century house and created an alternative entrance from the top of Ballards Way, erecting a lodge at each entrance. In May 1919 Howard Houlder, the shipping magnate and mayor of Croydon during the First World War, bought the estate for £30,000. In 1927 Raymond Riesco then purchased Heathfield, establishing the ornamental gardens with its walled garden, terraces, rock garden and displays of rhododendron and azaleas and pulled down the west wing. The attached farm was leased to Peter Thrale who bred racehorses.

The staff at Heathfield under Henry Goschen, taken in the 1890s. The group includes Joseph Hill, the farm's stockman, seen standing in the centre wearing an Arum Lily buttonhole. The lady seated first left was Mrs Appleby, the coachman's wife.

In December 1945 Raymond Riesco entered into an agreement with Croydon Corporation under which the latter would buy the estate for £83,000. Monks Hill, part of the farm, was bought immediately and developed for housing and schools with the remainder to be bought when Riesco wished to sell. He died in March 1964 and, as agreed, the Corporation purchased the rest of the estate and opened the grounds to the public. As part of another agreement, Riesco made a gift of his oriental china, provided the collection was not split up. This can now be seen at the Riesco Gallery within the Croydon Clocktower library and museum complex. His daughter, Jean Riesco, is driving the tractor.

The Valve House 1906. Housing the valves for Addington Reservoir built on the southern side of Addington Hills in 1888, the Valve House became a particular attraction as it had a tea-room serving refreshments on the ground floor. Unfortunately, a typhoid outbreak in Croydon in 1937 was traced back to the reservoir and as a consequence the area was fenced off.

Broadcoombe Cottage on a snowy day in April 1908 stood on the north-east side of Coombe Lane on the edge of Addington Hills. It probably dated from the early nineteenth century. Shown on a map of Broad Coombe Farm, 1832, as Bryant's cottage it later became the gardener's cottage of Coombe House. It had also been named Boundary Cottage as part of the garden was in Addington Parish while the building was in Croydon Parish.

Broadcoombe Cottage, photographed in 1923, was occupied for many years by W.H. Mills who moved there in 1899, six years after his marriage to Emma, seen on the right. Always known as 'Peter' he developed a great interest in the local area. A well-known figure, he sang in the Addington church choir. On his death in 1951, aged eighty-one, his papers and drawings were donated to the Croydon Reference Library. The girl in black is his eldest daughter and her friend on the left is Ethel Martin.

Until the Reformation, Ballards was in the possession of the Priory of St Mary Overie, Southwark, and was known as Prior Ballards. It then passed to the Leigh family who owned the whole of Addington until the eighteenth century. Charles Hermann Goschen bought it in 1872 and built a new mansion on the summit of the hill. The original mansion, situated in the valley below, was then demolished. In 1920 Howard Houlder then bought Ballards. Soon after, Houlder sold the estate to Mr H. Hollingsworth of Bourne & Hollingsworth department store who presented the estate to the Trustees of the Warehousemen, Drapers' and Haberdashers' school, who were looking for a new site for the school.

Charles Hermann Goschen, seen sitting outside Ballards with his wife Helen, was born in January 1839, one of a number of sons of William Henry Goschen. A noted financier of his day, C.H. Goschen became Lord Lieutenant of the City of London and also director of the Bank of England. His eldest brother, George, served as Chancellor of the Exchequer in Lord Salisbury's second government and was created Viscount Goschen in 1900. Charles Goschen died on 22 March 1915.

Nestling below Bramley Bank, No. 39 Chapel View was the residence of Henry Grantham, gamekeeper of the Ballards estate. Without the 1930s housing development one can imagine the perfect view overlooking the Croham Valley. Access to the house was by a track leading from the lane to Ballards Farm. Henry and his wife Sarah came from the Dorking area in about 1890 and worked at Ballards until at least 1910.

The second Ballards Farm in August 1926, built during the ownership of Ballards by C.H. Goschen. The original farm stood just to the east along the present Ballards Way, behind the yellow-brick wall which enclosed the farm. Leading off Ballards Way today is Hollingsworth Road, named after Mr H. Hollingsworth, one of the earlier benefactors of Royal Russell school. Many of the farm buildings were destroyed in a fire in 1914.

A mock up of the Seven Dwarfs cottage was erected at Ballards Farm as part of the advertising for the showing of the newly-released Walt Disney cartoon *Snow White and the Seven Dwarfs* being shown at the Davis Theatre in Croydon from 26 September 1938.

Changes in the education system and the effects of the First World War created pressure on accommodation at the Warehousemen, Clerks and Drapers' schools at Russell Hill, Purley. A new site was deemed necessary. A committee set up by Mr E.R. Debenham and Mr W.W. Bourne of Bourne & Hollingsworth fame were instructed to find a new site for the school. Through the generosity of Mr H. Hollingsworth, Ballards was purchased from the then owner, Howard Houlder, at a price of £21,000. At first, the boys of the school moved to Ballards, the first group moving there in May 1921. Ballards mansion was not the complete answer to the school's needs so the architect, Sir Aston Webb (noted for Admiralty Arch, Imperial College of Science and the Victoria & Albert Museum) was appointed to design the new school. His plans are well illustrated here in this aerial view of the estate taken in 1924, revealing Aston's design consisting of three blocks forming an H.

The original school at Russell Hill, Purley, had no chapel of its own, so the plans for the new school included a chapel which would commemorate those school members who had died in the First World War. The Prince of Wales laid the foundation stone on 23 July 1924 while the consecration and dedication to St Christopher took place two years later on 26 May 1926. The tower, with the clock and chimes, commemorating the fifty years service the first Lord Hollenden completed as treasurer of the school, is a local landmark and the chimes can be heard for some distance around.

Opposite below: The middle block as originally planned consisted of two dormitories with bedrooms for the masters; matron's rooms and the sick bay lay between them. An open cloister joined all three sections, while the main entrance was the large portico facing out on to the quadrangle with Ballard's mansion on the opposite side. This block is now known as Oxford House, photographed in November 1972.

Sports Day at the school in 1930 with the mayor and mayoress, Alderman and Mrs T.A. Lewis, standing in the middle of this group. With the mayor are Dr and Mrs John Newnham.

The visit by Her Majesty the Queen to the school in a blizzard on 23 March 1979. The Queen, as Princess Elizabeth, had first visited the school on 11 February 1950 and even that visit took place in atrocious weather. Her Majesty conferred the title 'Royal' upon the school in 1953 in honour of the school's centenary. By an Act of Parliament in 1963 the school became officially Royal Russell school and in 2003 will celebrate its sesquicentenary.

The Mayor's Garden Party held at Coombe Wood on Wednesday, 27 June 1951. The young girl next to the Bishop of Croydon, Rt Revd Cuthbert Bardsley, is Jennifer Marshall, daughter of Alderman James Marshall. Behind is Coombe Wood House built in 1898 for Arthur Lloyd, brother of Frank Lloyd. He installed a three manual Lewis church organ, with the keyboard in the main entrance hall and the pipes fitting into the staircase panelling. After the death of Arthur Lloyd in 1911 William Cash, later to become chairman of the Croydon Gas Company, purchased the house. Cash arranged to sell Coombe Wood House and its grounds to Croydon Corporation and since then the house has had a succession of uses including spells as a convalescent home, a children's home and now a popular restaurant, The Chateau. The ornamental grounds and fourteen acres of woodland were opened to the public in 1948.

John Kennedy, a well-known person in Coombe at the end of the nineteenth century, was bailiff to Herbert Lloyd at Coombe Farm from 1893 to 1901. On the death of Herbert Lloyd, Kennedy moved first to Reading then rented a dairy farm near Handcross in Sussex. Note the buttoned leather gaiters which Kennedy is wearing.

Coombe is the name of an ancient estate first recorded in 1221. In the time of Elizabeth I it was known as Broad Coombe. In the seventeenth century, Coombe was owned by Matthew and Daniel Harvey, brothers of William Harvey who discovered the circulation of the blood. Coombe Lodge, once Coombe Gate (or Green) House, is a red-brick, Georgian mansion built before 1756. The building was originally a cube but had extensions added both east and south. In 1761 the estate was sold to James Bourdieu who also owned nearby Coombe House and Coombe Farm. The original combined estate of Coombe was divided and united a number of times. One owner, Ashley Cronmire, who lived at Coombe Lodge from 1893 to 1897, added the fine conservatory at its western end. Here in 1934 a garden party is taking place in the grounds of Coombe Lodge then in the occupancy of Sir Herbert Browne, a colleague of Earl Haig.

An interior view taken in 1912 of one of the principal rooms of Coombe Lodge. After the Second World War, Croydon Corporation bought the property, established the Central Nursery of Croydon Parks Department in the grounds and opened the building as an old peoples' home. The home closed in 1988 and the future of Coombe Lodge was in doubt. However, the house has since become a restaurant presently owned by the Out & Out restaurant chain.

A little way beyond Coombe, back towards Croydon, two thatched lodges stood at the entrance to a path leading from Coombe Lane to Croham House and Farm. These buildings, known as Croham Lodges, were demolished in 1902 when the houses in Coombe Lane, later Coombe Road, Campden Road and Croham Park Avenue were constructed. The path still exists as a right of way behind the houses in Campden Road.

Coombe House in 1909. A house has stood on this site since the latter half of the sixteenth century. Coombe House was built by James Bourdieu in 1761 shortly after his purchase of the estate of Coombe having demolished the previous building. Soon after 1830 the then owner, Mr J.W. Sutherland, made a number of alterations to the property, giving it the appearance seen here in this photograph. On the death of Mrs Sutherland in 1892 it was purchased by Frank Lloyd, the newspaper magnate, who made further alterations to the property. Coombe House has since been renamed Geoffrey Harris House and is now in the possession of the Lifecare NHS Trust.

Pilgrim's Well, once in the grounds of Coombe House, but now within the garden of a more recent house of the same name. Over 145 feet deep, tradition says that pilgrims on their way to Canterbury could do no better than travel via the Archbishop's Palace in Croydon, then proceed to Coombe for refreshment. In 1897 Mr Frank Lloyd rediscovered the well and added the ornate stone and iron top. An icehouse also exists in the grounds.

Coombe Farm, seen here around 1890, is reached down Oaks Lane from Oaks Road. The earliest portion of the range of buildings is the low, two-storied farmhouse facing south, probably dating from the late sixteenth century. In 1844 further rooms were added to the north of the original Tudor property forming the present roofline. In 1893 Herbert Lloyd, brother of Frank Lloyd, erected a much larger building with many mock-Tudor features, attached at right angles to the rear of the original farmhouse. For many years a home run by the charity Scope, Coombe Farm is now in use as a hostel.

An early nineteenth-century, weather-boarded cottage in Oaks Lane belonging to Oaks Farm, an ancient estate once belonging to the Archbishops of Canterbury and the home farm to Shirley House. Its fields lay to the south of Oaks Lane. John Maberly, of Shirley House, who leased the farm from 1803, was allowed to close Oaks Lane as a public road (it is a path open to the public but with no actual right of way) having paid for the making up of Oaks Road instead. Oaks Lane leads back to Shirley Park.

Acknowledgements

The pictures appearing in this book have come from various sources and collections, including my own. I am grateful to those who have lent them or given me permission for their pictures to be reproduced:

Joe Baxter (Shirley Methodist church); Liz Bebbington (All Saints church, Spring Park); Albert Bennett; Gerry Coll; Croydon Natural History & Scientific Society; Mr J.M. Haybittle; David Hunt; John Gent; *Croydon Advertiser*; Pam Hooks (St George's church, Shirley); Jane Marchini; David Matthews (Shirley Park Golf Club); Jim Richards (St. Edward's church, New Addington); Susan Powell (St John's Church of England school); Christina Smith (7th Shirley, All Saints, Guides); and Ian Wiltshire.

The following photographs have come from the collection belonging to the Croydon Local Studies Library: Page 4, 9, 10a, 11a, 12b, 14b, 16b, 17, 18a, 20, 22, 24ab, 25, 26b, 27ab, 28a, 29, 33b, 39ab, 40, 41ab, 43a, 44ab, 46b, 47b, 48, 49, 51, 52ab, 53a, 54, 57ab, 60ab, 61a, 63b, 64ab, 65ab, 66ab, 68ab, 69, 70, 71ab, 76ab, 78, 81, 82b, 83ab, 84a, 85b, 87b, 88, 90ab, 91b, 92ab, 93, 95b, 97b, 98ab, 99ab, 100ab, 103, 104ab, 106ab, 107a, 111ab, 112a, 113, 114ab, 116ab, 117, 118ab, 119ab, 120a, 121a, 122a, 123ab, 124, 125ab, 126ab,127a. Bethlem Royal Hospital Archives and Museum: Page 73b. London Transport Museum: Page 77. Omnibus Society: Page 107b. Realistic: Page 112b. Simmons Aerofilms Ltd: Page 105.

My sincere thanks must go to Daphne Hillyer for her enthusiasm which helped me commence writing the book, as well as all those Shirley residents who have offered encouragement along the way. I am also extremely grateful for the support of the many people who have contributed in one way or another in the production of this book including Steve Roud, Chris Bennett, Christine Corner, Christine Smith and all the staff at Croydon Local Studies Library for their support and use of facilities; to Gerry Coll and Eileen Loydd for their encouragement; and my colleagues at the Open University in London. Finally, I am indebted to my wife, Susan, for her support throughout by proof-reading and correcting the captions and for offering her valued advice.

Children of Addington Village school photographed in the field adjoining Upper Farm, *c.* 1907. Entries in school logbooks indicate that during the shooting season boys were employed by the landowners of the district to bag game or act as beaters; an aspect of rural Addington now gone.